GREGORIO ESPARZA
ALAMO DEFENDER

WILLIAM R. CHEMERKA
ILLUSTRATIONS BY
DON COLLINS

Dedicated to the descendants of Gregorio Esparza

bright sky press
HOUSTON, TEXAS

bright sky press
HOUSTON, TEXAS

2365 Rice Boulevard, Suite 202,
Houston, Texas 77005

10   9   8   7   6   5   4   3   2   1
Library of Congress Cataloging-in Publication Data

Chemerka, William R.
Gregorio Esparza : Alamo defender / by William R. Chemerka ; Illustrated by Don Collins.
p. cm. -- (Texas heroes for young readers ; 3)
Includes index.
ISBN 978-1-933979-36-6 (hardcover : alk. paper)
1. Esparza, Gregorio, 1808-1836--Juvenile literature. 2. Alamo (San Antonio, Tex.)--Siege,
1836--Biography--Juvenile literature. 3. Pioneers--Texas--Biography--Juvenile literature.
I. Collins, Don, ill. II. Title. III. Series.

F390.E87C45 2009
976.4'03--dc22

2009007340

Book and cover design by Cregan Design
Illustrated by Don Collins
Printed in China through Asia Pacific Offset

ACKNOWLEDGEMENTS

Thanks to George Benavides, a descendant of Gregorio Esparza, for his assistance, encouragement and friendship.

I appreciate the helpful efforts of Cory Morales, who is also a descendant of Gregorio Esparza.

Thanks also to Elaine Davis and Martha Utterback of the Daughters of the Republic of Texas (DRT) Library at the Alamo for their assistance. Of particular importance at the DRT Library was information provided by the late Reynaldo J. Esparza, a descendant of Gregorio Esparza.

I am most grateful to Enrique Esparza, the son of Gregorio Esparza, who provided important details about his family and the Battle of the Alamo in early 20th century newspaper interviews conducted by Charles Merritt Barnes of the *San Antonio Express*. Esparza was the oldest survivor of the Siege and Battle of the Alamo to provide details about the legendary mission-fortress in 1836. Alejo Perez, who was an infant in the Alamo at the time, was the last survivor of the Alamo battle. However, Perez was too young to recall anything about Texas' most memorable event as an adult.

Finally, thanks to the staff of Bright Sky Press for presenting the story of Gregorio Esparza to a new generation of young readers.

William R. Chemerka

TABLE OF CONTENTS

CHAPTER 1

....

Prologue

1835

Gregorio Esparza lived in San Antonio, Texas under three different flags.

He was born under the flag of Spain on February 25, 1802.

When he was nineteen, the flag of Mexico became his national banner. And at age thirty-four, Gregorio Esparza fought for the flag that flew over the Alamo.

Mexico won its independence from Spain in 1821. The Mexicans were proud of their freedom. Three years later, the new nation created a constitution modeled after the United States Constitution. Like the United States, the citizens of Mexico would be able to elect their leaders.

Coahuila y Tejas was the name given to the Mexican state that included what is now Texas. The citizens of Coahuila y Tejas and the other states were allowed to send their own representatives to Mexico City, the capital of the new nation.

In the 1820s, Mexico was primarily a nation of farmers. The members of the Esparza family were farmers, too. Juan Antonio Esparza and his wife, Petra, had six children. Their youngest was José Gregorio Esparza. They called him Gregorio.

As a young boy, Gregorio worked with his older brothers

and sister on the family farm. Their main crop was corn. By their hard work, the Esparzas managed to provide ample food for themselves. They would sometimes trade their extra corn for pigs and chickens. They lived a simple but enjoyable life in San Antonio de Béxar.

Gregorio grew up to be a strong young man. He met and fell in love with Ana Salazar. Ana was a widow and had a daughter, Maria. They later married and had four children: José, Enrique, Manuel and Francisco. But José died of illness at age three.

Like his parents, Gregorio was a farmer. He worked very hard on the small plot of land that he owned. As his children grew, they helped him on the farm. But he wanted more for his children. He wanted them to get an education. He wanted them to be successful.

The Mexican government encouraged Americans to settle in Mexico. Mexico offered large land grants to the Americans if they promised to become Mexican citizens, join the Catholic church and pledge not to bring in slaves.

To many Americans, Texas was a land of opportunity. Thousands were attracted by the generous land offer and soon settled in Texas. "Gone to Texas" was what they told their former neighbors back in the United States. The Anglo immigrants called themselves Texians or Texans. The native-born Mexicans in Texas called themselves Tejanos.

Like the Tejanos, the Anglo immigrants worked hard setting up their farms and cattle ranches. Texas became a popular place to live. Soon, there were more Anglos living in

Texas than Tejanos.

The Mexican government limited American immigration in 1830. Later, General Santa Anna became President of Mexico. He did not follow the laws of the Constitution of 1824 and ended representative government, people governed by the people. As a result local leaders like Stephen Austin and Juan Seguin protested his rule. But some other Mexican citizens supported Santa Anna.

At first, Gregorio Esparza did not want to get involved in the growing protests against Santa Anna. But he realized that Santa Anna stood in the way of freedom for all Mexicans, whether Anglo or Tejano. And he wanted his children to live in a free country, a nation where the people—not General Santa Anna—ruled.

Santa Anna wanted to make sure that the protests did not grow into a rebellion. He ordered the arrest of some people and planned to take away the weapons of others.

In October of 1835, Santa Anna ordered his soldiers to take a cannon that was in the town of Gonzales. But when his soldiers showed up they were met by a group of citizens carrying a flag that said "Come And Take It." They fired their guns at the advancing Mexican soldiers and chased them from Gonzales. The first battle of the Texas Revolution had been fought.

Later in October, some Texans planned to take the Mexican fort at Goliad.

CHAPTER 2

The Ride to Goliad

October 1835

Gregorio Esparza finished saddling his horse.

He adjusted his blanket roll, pressed the cork stopper firmly into his gourd canteen, and mounted the horse. He held his rifle in one hand and the reins in the other. Then he looked at his house where his wife and children stood near the doorway.

His wife, Ana, walked up to him and grasped his hand. Her eyes filled with tears.

"Gregorio."

"Do not worry about me, Ana," Gregorio said with a reassuring smile.

"Why do you have to go?" she asked.

"All the men are going. We have spoken many times about this day. And now that day is here."

"But why you, Gregorio?"

"Our country is based on freedom. The Constitution of 1824 says so. But General Santa Anna has taken our freedoms away and we must fight to get them back."

He leaned down from the saddle and faced his children.

"Now then, Enrique, Manuel, Francisco, listen to your mother while I am gone. And listen to your sister, Maria, too. Enrique, you are my oldest son, so I am depending on you."

"Yes, Father."

"You are a fine young man."

Enrique stood erect like a soldier at attention and raised a wooden toy pistol that his father had carved for him as a birthday gift.

"Gregorio…" said Ana. But she could not finish what she wanted to say.

"Don't worry. I will be fine."

"But what will I tell them if you do not return?" said Ana softly so the children would not hear.

"Tell them that their father fought for freedom."

Gregorio Esparza spurred his horse and quickly rode off.

He rode past the Alamo, the old Spanish mission that was located near his home in San Antonio. Then he continued along the road to Goliad, the place where he was going to join some of the other men of his community in a fight against Santa Anna's soldiers.

But after only a few miles he saw several men armed with muskets ambling towards him from a rise near the road. Gregorio pulled his horse up and looked carefully at them.

"Gregorio!" yelled one of them.

He quickly recognized the men in the group. They were his neighbors, including his good friends Toribio Losoya and Juan Abamillo.

"Toribio!" he shouted.

"Gregorio!"

Gregorio rode ahead to meet them. He pulled up his horse as a cloud of dust kicked up from the road.

"Toribio, Goliad is that way," said Gregorio and he pointed in the direction from which the men had come. "You are going the wrong way."

"No, Gregorio, you are going the wrong way. It's over. The fighting is over. We have won!"

"What do you mean?"

"We have taken Presidio la Bahia," said Toribio as the others congratulated each other with pats on the back and laughter. "Santa Anna's soldiers are gone. We have fought for the Constitution, and we've won!"

"You certainly didn't need my help," joked Gregorio. "Were there any casualties?"

"We did not lose a man," said Juan.

"That is good."

"And when does a farmer like you, Gregorio, have a fine horse such as this?" asked Toribio with a wide smile.

"It belongs to all the members of the Esparza family," grinned Gregorio.

"All the members?" said Toribio.

"Yes, all," replied Gregorio.

"Even your brother, Francisco?" said Juan.

"Even Francisco," said Gregorio.

"But Francisco serves in the army of Santa Anna," said Toribio.

"I know that, but he is still my brother."

"And what if one day you were to face him on the battlefield?"

Gregorio stopped smiling for a moment. He thought

carefully about what Toribio had said. But a grin soon returned to his face.

"Didn't you say the fighting was over?" asked Gregorio.

They all looked at each other and smiled. And the smiles once again turned to laughter. In less than an hour after he left for Goliad, Gregorio was home having supper with his family.

"I did not know I would be home so soon," said Gregorio.

"We are glad you are safe with us, Father," said Maria.

"Are you going to have another fight with the soldiers?" asked Enrique.

"Hush now," said Ana.

"Are you, Father?" said Enrique as he walked up to his father and stood next to him.

"You are nearly as tall as I am when I sit on my bench," said Gregorio.

Enrique knew that his father was trying to change the conversation to something other than fighting. Enrique waited for an answer.

"No, my son. No more fighting. Now finish your supper."

But Ana wasn't convinced by his reply. Gregorio knew that she was still concerned about the possibility of more fighting.

The children helped their mother clean the table. Then they quickly ran outside to play in the garden while light still glimmered from the setting sun. Ana placed the last dinner bowl on a shelf and sat at the table next to her husband.

"Gregorio, is the fighting really over?

"For now, yes."

"For now?"

"I fear that the fighting may begin again," said Gregorio.

"Again? Where?"

"Perhaps here in San Antonio."

"Gregorio, no one would be foolish enough to attack General Cós."

"He has the only sizeable force of Santa Anna's soldiers in Texas. Once they are removed, our freedoms will be returned."

"Whose freedoms? The Anglo settlers' freedoms or ours?" said Ana.

"Anglo or Tejano, we are all Texans," said Gregorio. "We want our representative government back. We want our freedoms. And some of us are willing to fight for them."

"General Cós is in our community," said Ana. "His soldiers are everywhere. Your brother, Francisco, is one of them. We will be the ones who will have to pay the price for all of this one day."

"The Anglos have paid, too."

"How?"

"Stephen Austin, Will Travis, Ben Milam and others have been placed in jail for speaking out against Santa Anna," said Gregorio as he stood up and walked to the window where he could see his children.

"Imagine that, Ana. They were placed in a jail for simply speaking. In years to come, can you imagine our children being sent to a jail for speaking the truth."

Ana walked next to him and saw the children playing. They were having a wonderful time.

"Perhaps Toribio is correct," said Gregorio. "Maybe the fighting is over."

CHAPTER 3

....

The Texas Revolution

October/November 1835

But the fighting continued.

On October 12, the Texans began a siege against San Antonio. Under the command of Stephen Austin, the armed force attempted to surround the town in order to prevent any Mexican reinforcements from reaching General Cós and his soldiers.

Austin planned to attack General Cos' main army in early December. The Mexican soldiers were scattered throughout San Antonio and the Alamo, which was located across the San Antonio River from the town.

Austin formed infantry, artillery and cavalry companies. Juan Seguin, another friend of Gregorio's, was given command of the Tejano cavalry companies.

Gregorio Esparza was still at home. He stared aimlessly at the back wall of the kitchen as his family ate breakfast.

"Father," said Enrique. "Father?"

"Oh, I am sorry, my son," said Gregorio. "I was just thinking."

"Something about Juan Seguin's visit last night?' asked Ana as she spooned out another serving of potatoes to the children.

Gregorio sat silently as his children finished their breakfast.

"Tomorrow is the first day of December," said Maria. "Christmas will soon be here." The Esparza children smiled with glee.

"Will you carve another pistol for me, Father?" said Enrique.

"Enough of you," said Ana. "Time to feed the chickens. Out you go."

The children laughed as they left the kitchen.

"Christmas should be a time of peace, but the fighting goes on," said Ana.

"It will be a time of peace when all of this is over," said Gregorio.

"And when will that be?"

"Soon. Very soon. Juan Seguin is leading a force of Tejano volunteers against General Cós."

"Here?" asked Ana. "Here, in San Antonio? The siege is bad enough. The soldiers are everywhere. They look at us and worry if we are friend or foe, and we look at them in the same way."

"They are not our friends," said Gregorio. "When we rid this place of General Cós' soldiers we will have a Christmas that we will all enjoy,"

"All of his soldiers?" asked Ana.

"Of course."

"Including Francisco?" asked Ana.

"My brother serves in the army of Cós but he will not fight against his own family," said Gregorio.

"And how sure are you of that?" said Ana.

Suddenly, Enrique ran back in the kitchen.

"Uncle Francisco is coming," announced Enrique.

Gregorio and Ana walked to the front door. The children soon followed.

Francisco Esparza was wearing his Mexican Army uniform but he did not carry his weapons. As he approached the house he removed his hat.

"Good morning, Ana."

"Good morning, Francisco."

"And a good morning to you, children. A very good morning!"

Francisco gently patted each one of them on their heads. The children smiled.

"A fine family, my brother. And they grow bigger each day."

For several moments everyone just stood there. Then Enrique took a step towards his uncle.

"Uncle Francisco, are you going to fight Father?" asked Enrique.

"Nephew, why would you say something like that?" said Francisco as he placed his hat on Enrique's head.

Ana placed her arm around Enrique and looked directly at Francisco. Gregorio removed the hat from his son's head and gave it back to Francisco.

"We need to talk," said Francisco to Gregorio.

Ana quickly escorted the children back into the house and then returned to the men.

"Remember, you are more than just brothers," she

pleaded. "Francisco, you are my brother-in-law, the uncle to my children. Please remember that." She turned and entered the house.

"The siege continues but it does not affect General Cós," said Francisco.

"I have heard otherwise," said Gregorio.

"From who, Juan Seguin?" asked Francisco.

"You know of Juan?" asked Gregorio.

"We know he is a pirate, a rebel Texan, one who breaks the laws of Mexico," said Francisco.

"General Santa Anna breaks the laws of Mexico," said Gregorio. "He has cast aside the freedoms we enjoyed under the Constitution."

"Oh, my brother, why do you speak such treason?"

"Treason, you say?"

"Indeed, Gregorio." Francisco placed his right hand on Gregorio's shoulder and smiled. "Look, my brother, I know you ride with the pirate, Seguin. But if you stop now, I will never tell of your treason. And nothing will happen to you."

"And if I do not?" asked Gregorio.

Francisco removed his hand from Gregorio's shoulder and placed his hat back on his head. He placed the chin strap firmly in place.

"We know that Stephen Austin has left for the United States," said Francisco as he grasped the reins of the horse. "He has been replaced by Edward Burleson, another Anglo. It is the Anglos that have caused all of this. And you will pay the price, my brother."

"Francisco, listen to me," said Gregorio in a very serious tone. "Anglos and Tejanos want the same freedoms. And we are willing to fight for them. Together."

For several moments both brothers looked at each other and said nothing. There was silence except for the sounds of the Esparza children who were at play behind the nearby houses.

"Adios, Gregorio."

"Adios, Francisco."

Francisco turned and walked away.

In the days that followed, Gregorio and his family anxiously waited for word of the attack against General Cós. They did not have to wait long.

On the night of December 3, Juan Seguin returned to Gregorio's house and told him to report to an area outside of the town where General Burleson was forming the Texans in preparation for an attack. General Burleson had replaced Stephen Austin as the commander.

At home, Gregorio looked in on his sleeping children.

"It is time to go, Ana," he whispered

"Come back to us safe and sound," said Ana.

"I will," Gregorio reassured her as he left the house and mounted his horse.

Gregorio smiled at Ana as he galloped north. Before long he saw a row of campfires and hundreds of fellow volunteers. Toribio Losoya and Juan Abamillo greeted him.

"Gregorio!" shouted Toribio.

"It looks like I am not late this time," joked Gregorio.

Juan Seguin approached the group.

"My neighbors, my friends, it is time!" said Seguin. "Form your ranks!"

Gregorio and the rest of the men lined up

"This will be the fight that sends the last of Santa Anna's soldiers back beyond the Rio Grande," declared Toribio.

"Do not underestimate General Cós," cautioned Gregorio. "His men are ready to fight, too."

CHAPTER 4

....

The Battle of Bexar

December 1835

General Burleson stood near a campfire talking with his officers. Hundreds of volunteers were lined up around them. Gregorio and the other mounted scouts in Seguin's company stood by their horses.

General Burleson stepped away from his officers and faced the volunteers. "Men of Texas, it is time to send General Cós and his soldiers back to Mexico City," said the general. "It is time to restore the rights under the Constitution of 1824!"

Colonel Benjamin Milam stepped forward and shouted: "Who will go with old Ben Milam into San Antonio?"

A large cheer erupted from the volunteers.

General Burleson organized his attack force of over three hundred men into two groups, one commanded by Ben Milam and the other by Colonel Francis Johnson. A third group of reserves and scouts included Juan Seguin's volunteers.

Milam planned to begin his attack on San Antonio from a few small abandoned houses on the north side of town. Johnson's volunteers were positioned on his left. All the men were ready. Juan Abamillo reached into his saddle bag for some food. Toribio took a drink from his canteen. Gregorio examined his rifle.

Then they waited.

In the predawn darkness of the next morning, Colonel James Neill and his artillery crew positioned a cannon on the east bank of the San Antonio River facing the Alamo. At around five o'clock in the morning, Neill's men fired the cannon. The Battle of Bexar had begun.

Milam and Johnson's volunteers fired their muskets and rifles at the Mexican soldiers who were standing on guard duty. Quickly, additional Mexican soldiers emerged from their quarters and joined in the street fight.

Every house was important. The Texans had to take each structure in order to get closer to the town's Main Plaza. At first, General Cós thought the main attack was directed at the Alamo but he soon realized that his soldiers stationed in the town were the main target. He ordered his cannon crews on the Alamo's long west wall to fire into the town where the Texans could be seen.

A Mexican cannon ball blasted a large hole in a house not far from where Gregorio was positioned. Screams rang out from inside the battered home. A woman and her children quickly ran out the door. Gregorio immediately thought of his home and family on the other side of town. He hoped that the battle would not extend to every corner of San Antonio.

The street fighting was intense. Mexican soldiers had constructed barricades of lumber and carts on some of the streets. Other soldiers positioned themselves on rooftops. Inside many of the houses, Mexican soldiers fired out of partially opened windows and doors. The Texans fired back.

The fighting went on throughout the day and early evening.

Seguin's volunteers were positioned as reserves and had not yet participated in the battle. Each man fed and groomed his horse.

"When will they send us in?" asked Juan.

"Soon enough, Juan," said Gregorio. "Soon enough."

Darkness halted the battle. It was nearly impossible to see since every household lantern and candle was extinguished.

Juan Seguin addressed his volunteers.

"The battle has only begun," said Seguin. "I have been informed by General Burleson that we have lost only one man today."

"We are fortunate," said Gregorio.

A rider approached Seguin with orders.

"Mount up!" said Seguin. "Gen Cós will try to send out messengers tonight. And reinforcements may be on their way. It is our job to ride around the town and the Alamo to make sure no one gets in or out."

Gregorio exchanged looks of determination with Toribio and Juan. Seguin raised his arm and signaled. The mounted scouts followed him to the north side of town. Then they broke up into smaller groups. One group consisted of Gregorio, Toribio and Juan.

The three rode several hundred yards behind the rear of the Alamo church and positioned themselves in the tree-shaded alameda near the road to Gonzales. The trio could see the campfires built in the courtyard of the old mission fortress.

~ 27 ~

"Looks peaceful," said Juan.

"For tonight, perhaps," said Gregorio. A moment later, Gregorio's horse grew restless.

"She must not like you anymore?" laughed Toribio.

"Quiet," said Gregorio. "Look. Over there."

Gregorio pointed to the Alamo's main gate where a Mexican cavalryman trotted his horse out into the darkness towards the road.

"He won't get through our lines," said Gregorio as he spurred his horse. "Let's ride!"

Gregorio and his companions rode towards the cavalryman. Musket fire erupted from the walls of the Alamo as the three approached. The rider hesitated when Gregorio came into view. The musket fire increased but the shots missed. The startled rider made a sudden turn back into the fort.

Gregorio's group stopped as a few musket balls whizzed past them.

"Come on then," said Gregorio. The three spurred their horses and returned to the safety of the alameda.

"That was a close call," said Juan.

"Too close," said Gregorio as he took Toribio's hat off his head and showed him the musket ball hole in the brim. Toribio looked surprised as he stuck his finger through the hole in his hat.

Several minutes later Juan Seguin rode up.

"What happened?" asked Seguin.

"Cós sent out a rider," said Gregorio.

"But Gregorio chased him back," said Toribio.

"We all chased him back," said Gregorio. "It was not only me."

"Good work," said Seguin. "But Cós will try again. Be on your guard until sunrise, amigos."

CHAPTER 5

The Artillerist

December 1835

At dawn, Seguin addressed his scouts.

"Although we lost but one man yesterday, fifteen men have been wounded. Some of them were the artillerists who loaded and fired the cannons," said Seguin. "We need replacements for them. Does any man have any artillery experience?"

No one replied.

"Well, then," said Seguin, "do any of you want to volunteer to serve on the cannons?"

Gregorio stepped forward.

"Gregorio are you trying to get killed?" said Toribio.

"Report to Colonel Neill," ordered Seguin.

"Yes, sir," said Gregorio.

Gregorio handed the reins of his horse to Toribio and walked to Colonel Neill's headquarters. A guard stopped him.

"Halt!" said the guard.

"I'm the new gunner," said Gregorio.

"Oh," said the guard. "Did you ever serve on a cannon?"

"No," said Gregorio. "But I am willing to learn."

"They will be no artillery lessons right now. The crews are asleep. It's been a long day for them. So go find some place to bed down nearby. My relief will wake you up later."

Gregorio walked inside an abandoned building that only had half a roof. He curled up on the floor. His hunting bag served as a pillow. At first he could not fall asleep. He kept thinking about the safety of his family. Eventually, he fell asleep. But he did not get to sleep long.

"Wake up," said the sentry

Gregorio opened his eyes. He felt as if he had only slept for a few minutes.

"What time is it?" asked Gregorio.

"Time for your lesson."

An officer walked in.

"You are Esparza? Gregorio Esparza?"

Gregorio nodded as he stood.

"I am Colonel Neill and I want to thank you for volunteering to serve on one of our artillery crews. First, let's get you fed and then we'll begin."

Gregorio followed Colonel Neill to a campfire where beans and bread were served. Gregorio ate quickly. He could see the faint light of sunrise in the east.

"An artillerist is not like an individual rifleman who acts on his own," said Neill. "He is part of a team that works together. Let me show you."

Neill signaled to a group of men who stood by a nearby cannon. Each man was positioned at a specific place around the gun.

"Load!" shouted Neill.

As the men sprang to action, Neill described what each man was doing.

"The first man searches the barrel and removes any remnants of the previously fired charge. Then the gunner with the leather thumbstall on his hand seals the touch hole. The other gunner swabs the piece with the wet lamb's wool sponge. He extinguishes any sparks from the previous shot. We don't want the cannon to fire prematurely or our own men will be hurt. Now listen."

A thumping pop sounded as the gunner removed the ram sponge.

"That's the air rushing back into the barrel. The barrel is clean and awaits the charge," said Neill.

A member of the gun crew walked from behind the cannon and handed a solid iron ball attached to a bag of gunpowder to the man who searched the barrel. The man quickly inserted the charge into the muzzle of the cannon. The man who sponged the barrel used the other end of his staff to push the charge down the barrel.

"The gunner with the thumbstall inserts a metal vent pick down the touch hole to open up the powder bag," said Neill. "He then adds some gunpowder to the touch hole."

"Prime!" shouted the gunner.

"That's the only thing you will hear in the field," said Neill. "Once the gun is primed, it is ready to fire. And make sure you step back away from the wheels. That gun will recoil right on your feet if you're not careful."

Another gunner with a lighted linstock on a short staff ignited the touch hole charge. The cannon fired with a loud blast.

"Good morning, General Cós!" shouted Neill. The men cheered. He turned to Gregorio.

"The gun that you will serve on is closer to the river," said Neill. "You will serve as the gunner who sponges and loads. Follow the sergeant and he will lead you there. Good luck."

"Thank you, sir," said Gregorio. "I will do my best."

Mexican artillery from the Alamo started firing as Gregorio made his way to his cannon position. Rifles and muskets fired, too.

Gregorio arrived at the cannon, grabbed the sponge-ram staff and took his position near the muzzle of the cannon.

"You know what to do now?" asked the gun's officer.

"Yes, sir,"

"Load!" shouted the officer.

Gregorio quickly sprang in to action. He placed the sponge end of the staff into a bucket of water and swabbed the barrel. A few seconds later the charge was placed just inside the muzzle and Gregorio rammed the charge. He removed the rammer, stepped back and waited for the cannon to be primed.

An instant after the priming charge was ignited the cannon fired. It was the loudest noise that Gregorio had ever heard. White smoke filled the air.

CHAPTER 6

....

Fighting in the Streets

December 1835

Fighting continued for several days in the streets of San Antonio.

While Gregorio served on one of the cannons, the other volunteers continued the house-to-house fighting. The Texans couldn't enter well-defended house entrances so they used tools to break holes in the walls of the buildings. Rifle and musket barrels fired through tiny openings in the rugged adobe walls. An occasional cannon blast added to the frightful sounds of battle. The fighting was intense and casualties mounted on both sides. Ben Milam was shot and killed on the afternoon of December 7. A cold rain followed that night and the fighting stopped. Soldiers on both sides sought the protection of nearby houses. Seguin's mounted scouts continued their patrols but found it difficult to see beyond a hundred feet or so.

Gregorio and the other artillerists huddled under a thatched overhang next to a house which protected them and their cannon.

"It's good to be out of the rain," said a cannoneer from Kentucky. "But I'm soaked through."

"I wonder how many scouting patrols are riding tonight?" asked Gregorio as he shook the water from his hat.

"That's a miserable job on a night like this," said the

Kentuckian. "Let's go inside and build a fire."

The men found some wood stacked next to a small hearth. The Kentuckian used his tomahawk to make kindling from the wood. He carefully placed the wood in an organized pile and ignited the small splintered pieces with gunpowder from his flintlock pistol.

A tiny flame rose up from the stack of wood shavings.

"Ah, that's better," said Gregorio as he placed his hands over the fire.

Each man took turns standing near the small fire.

"All I need now is some beef," said the Kentuckian.

"And some corn bread with honey," said Gregorio.

Gradually, the topic of their conversation changed from food to politics.

"Some of us think that this fight is no longer about restoring rights under the Mexican Constitution of 1824," said the Kentuckian.

"What then?" asked Gregorio.

"New rights," said the Kentuckian. "Independence from Mexico. To be really free of Mexico City means to be independent."

"Independence, you say," said Gregorio as he moved closer to the fire. "That is a move that one should not make without careful consideration."

But think about it, Gregorio," said the Kentuckian. "An independent Texas."

A scout rode up to the building and quickly dismounted. "Mexican reinforcements just made it through our lines," said the rider. "They made it into the Alamo and they'll probably attack here once the rain stops. Colonel Neill says to get ready to move your cannon into position at the plaza."

The rain finally stopped at dawn. Gregorio and the others wheeled their cannon into a position near the Main Plaza, an area that was still held by the Mexican soldiers. Gregorio felt confident as a member of the crew. He carefully swabbed out the barrel and then rammed down charge after charge as the street fighting resumed.

The Mexicans fired back with artillery and musket fire but most of the Texans were well protected in their positions against the crumbled walls and abandoned buildings. A musket ball crashed into the cannon wheel and showered sharp splinters into Gregorio's coat. Another musket ball whizzed closely by his face but he remained at his post.

The volunteers moved closer to the fixed Mexican positions by gaining control of every nearby house. One by one, Mexican soldiers started to fall. The Mexicans were unable to halt the slow but steady Texan advance.

The next day, Gen. Cós ordered his men in the town to retreat back to the Alamo. General Burleson ordered his artillery to face the old mission. The Texans formed new positions near the Alamo's northern walls and main gate. Seguin's mounted Tejano scouts filled the area to the east. Cós was surrounded and his supplies were running low.

As night began to fall, Cós raised a flag of truce and sent an officer to discuss terms of surrender. The news spread quickly through the ranks of the Texans.

For the first time in nearly a week, all the guns were

silent. A lively party was celebrated in the streets. Gregorio was joined by Toribio and Juan.

"I am glad to see that you both are well," said Gregorio.

"And you, too," said Juan.

"My ears are still ringing from the cannon blasts," laughed Gregorio. "But I think I will get my best sleep in a week tonight." As he looked at the people celebrating he thought about what the Kentuckian had said about independence.

The next day, December 10, 1835, General Cós formally surrendered to General Burleson. The Mexican general promised to honor the Constitution of 1824 and not return. Hundreds of weapons were taken by the Texians and Tejanos including over twenty artillery pieces. Within a few days, Cós and his soldiers were on their way back across the Rio Grande. The local reserves, like Francisco Esparza, returned to their homes in the area.

A small Texan force remained in the Alamo but the rest of the men went home. Colonel Neill walked up to Gregorio and shook his hand.

"You did well, Esparza," said Neill.

"Thank you, sir."

"All my best to you and your family," said Neill. "I don't think you'll ever be firing a cannon again."

"Perhaps, Colonel," said Gregorio. "Adios."

"Adios."

CHAPTER 7

Home for the Winter

January 1836

The new year began peacefully.

Dozens of volunteers left for their homes. Only about one hundred remained with Colonel Neill, who was given the command of the Alamo.

On January 19, Colonel Jim Bowie and a group of volunteers entered the Alamo with orders from Sam Houston, the overall military leader of the Texans. They were ordered to destroy the Alamo and abandon it. But Bowie was impressed with the Alamo defenses. Bowie noticed that most of the Mexican cannons were still in good condition. Numerous Mexican muskets filled some of the Alamo's rooms. Bowie told Neill that the Alamo should not be abandoned.

However, some questioned Bowie's interest in fortifying the Alamo. After all, General Cós had left and promised never to return. The soldiers had left.

But what the Texans did not know was that Santa Anna was on his way to Texas. The Mexican dictator was determined to punish the rebels in San Antonio and everywhere else his authority was challenged.

Santa Anna led a force of some 6,000 soldiers in his Army of Operations towards the Rio Grande. The journey was extremely difficult for his men because the winter was terribly cold. Frequent ice and snow storms made it almost impossible to move at times. Still, they kept advancing towards San Antonio.

Most of the residents of San Antonio were content that the Battle of Bexar was just a memory. But inside the Esparza home, the fighting in December was still an exciting topic of discussion at nearly every family meal.

"Tell us again, Father," said Enrique from his usual position on the end of the bench nearest his mother at the kitchen table.

"Yes, tell us again," said Maria.

"Now then, my children, I can tell you about last month's battle only so many times," said Gregorio as he shared a smile with Ana.

"Will they soon make you a colonel, too?" asked Enrique.

"I don't think so," said Gregorio. "At least not this week."

"Enough of all this talk," said Ana. "General Cós is gone and that is all that matters."

"And Francisco no longer wears his uniform," said Gregorio. "That is good. He is a farmer once again like his brother."

"But I am still a soldier," said Enrique as he waved his toy pistol.

"General Enrique Esparza, finish your beans," said Ana.

"Yes, Mother," said Enrique.

"Maria, please bring back a pitcher of water to wash the dishes," said Ana. "And I want the rest of you to pull the bucket up from the well. Go now. Help your sister."

The children bounded out the rear door.

"It has been over a month since General Cós left," said Ana. "I am glad for all of us."

"I am glad for the children," said Gregorio.

Ana opened the curtains to let the morning sun pour in the room.

"When you were gone, we missed you very much."

"I know that, Ana."

"But we wanted to be with you."

"Ana, you can never think that way. It was much too dangerous."

"We could have stayed near you in some empty house."

"No, my dear. The walls of the houses did not offer protection from the cannons." Ana sat down next to Gregorio.

"Will General Cós return, Gregorio?"

"No, Ana. He will not return unless Santa Anna orders him back here."

"But he pledged not to return."

"Santa Anna would say that a pledge made to pirates is not a pledge at all," said Gregorio. "Do not worry, Ana. Even if Santa Anna wanted to, he could not."

"Why?"

"He would never send General Cós marching northward in the winter. That would be nearly impossible. After the arrival of the first ice, the soldiers, the horses, the cannons, would have to stop. Nothing could move."

Maria and her brothers returned with the water.

"It's so cold outside, Mother," said Maria.

"There was ice in the well," said Enrique. "We had to break it to get the water into the pitcher."

"Manuel and Francisco slipped on a patch of ice," said Maria.

Ana looked at Gregorio and smiled.

CHAPTER 8

Santa Anna Arrives

February 1836

Colonel Neill received information that Santa Anna had organized a large army in Saltillo, Mexico and was leading it against Texas strongholds in the north. Since Colonel Neill only had about one hundred volunteers inside the mission-fortress, he appealed for more help.

On February 3, William B. Travis arrived at the Alamo with a small company of men. But Neill needed more reinforcements. He wrote in a letter that he needed at least 600 volunteers.

Another small group arrived at the Alamo several days later and one of its members was none other than Davy Crockett, the famous frontier congressman from Tennessee. Word spread quickly of his arrival.

Gregorio was one of many townspeople who attended the fandango, a street dance held in Crockett's honor. Crockett told the crowd: "I have come to aid you all that I can in your noble cause." The crowd cheered.

Gregorio thought about the cause that Crockett had mentioned. Was it the struggle against Santa Anna to restore the Constitution or was it a fight for a total break from Mexico? Others in the crowd who remained loyal to Santa Anna looked on in silence.

John W. Smith, a San Antonio carpenter who had been

captured briefly by the Mexicans during the Battle of Bexar, was glad to see Gregorio.

"It is a day to behold," said Smith. "Davy Crockett is here in our own town!"

"Indeed," said Gregorio. "The congressman is well known and well liked by all."

"Not all, Gregorio."

Gregorio looked at his friend with a puzzled expression.

"There are many in this town who do not approve of anyone who stands against Santa Anna. And if the rumors are true that the general is coming here in the spring, we will be the ones who will be identified as rebels. And we will suffer the consequences."

"We defeated General Cós and we can defeat General Santa Anna," said Gregorio.

"I admire your confidence," said Smith. "But Santa Anna will bring ten times as many soldiers with him as General Cós. I know you do not worry about yourself but you have to take care of your family."

"That is a decision I will have to make when the time comes," said Gregorio.

"And that time may be here before you know it, my friend."

In the days that followed, additional volunteers slowly trickled in to San Antonio. However, Alamo commander Colonel Neill left for home on Feb. 14 to take care of sick family members. Gregorio had been trained by Neill to serve on the cannons. He was sad to see him go. Travis was put in command of the 150 men that made up the Alamo's garrison.

Despite the hard winter and the demanding journey, Santa Anna's army crossed the Rio Grande River on February 16. The large force included General Cós and his soldiers. Santa Anna's troops were only one week away from entering San Antonio.

During the next week, Gregorio tended to household chores. He first had to fix a broken leg on a bench that the children used at the breakfast table. Then he sharpened the tools he would need for spring planting. Enrique always worked alongside his father.

A knock at the door brought a stop to the chores. Enrique opened the door for John W. Smith.

"Good evening, Enrique," said Smith as he removed his stylish top hat. "Hello Ana, Gregorio."

"What brings you here so dressed up?" asked Ana.

"We're having another fandango tonight. We're celebrating George Washington's birthday, too. And Davy Crockett will be there, too. You folks coming?"

"You go, Gregorio," said Ana "I do not know of this Mr. Crockett or Mr. Washington. And it will be too cold tonight for the children to be outside."

Gregorio accompanied Smith to the party. When they arrived local musicians were playing songs while people danced in the streets. Many stood around Crockett as he told tall tales and lively frontier stories. Laughter filled the night.

Gregorio looked around and saw his brother, Francisco. He almost did not recognize him without his uniform.

Francisco seemed to be the only one who was not having a good time. But Gregorio and the others enjoyed the festivities. It was times like these that made San Antonio a wonderful place to live.

Smith suddenly reappeared.

"Gregorio, Santa Anna is only a day or two away," warned Smith.

"What? That cannot be. He could never have marched all that way in the winter."

"Gregorio, you and the other Tejanos who fought against General Cós will be in particular danger if Santa Anna takes San Antonio."

"I know, John. But I am more concerned about my wife and children. They will be safer in San Felipe. Good night, my friend."

Gregorio quickly walked home and told Ana what Smith had said.

On the next day, February 23, Travis ordered scouts to be placed in the San Fernando church bell tower to see if the rumors of Santa Anna's approach were true. The townspeople did not wait. Many packed their few belongings and quickly left their homes for the nearby roads that led to other settlements.

In the afternoon, a lookout in the bell tower shouted down that he saw the approach of soldiers. Travis sent riders out of the town to verify the report. Within minutes, the riders returned with shouts of "Santa Anna!"

Travis quickly ordered all under his command to run to

the Alamo for protection.

Gregorio was chopping firewood when Smith rode up. "Santa Anna! Just outside of town. Report to the Alamo. Now!"

Gregorio rushed back to his house.

"Santa Anna is coming. You and the children must depart now for San Felipe."

Ana clutched the children under her arms.

"We will not leave you this time, Gregorio."

"Please, Ana. We talked about this last night. I must report to Colonel Travis." He grabbed his musket and hunting bag and turned for the door.

"Then we will go with you," insisted Ana. "The walls of the church will protect us all."

Gregorio hesitated.

"All right, then," said Gregorio. "Get the children."

Gregorio led his family out the front door onto the street but Enrique pulled on his father's shirt.

"Wait!" said Enrique who ran back into the house. He returned moments later with his toy wooden pistol.

The nearby streets were filed with activity. Some families had placed their belongings on carts pulled by donkeys. Others carried their few possessions on their backs. But all wanted to avoid the upcoming battle. However, some, like Francisco Esparza, remained in their homes.

As Gregorio and his family approached the Alamo he saw that the main gate was crowded with riders and assorted volunteers carrying weapons and supplies. He

quickly directed his family along the south side of the Alamo church. He stopped at a partially blocked window and lifted each of his children through. He assisted Ana and then climbed in himself.

Inside, several Tejano families had gathered around an Anglo woman who held a young child. Gregorio guided his family to her.

"My name is Susanna Dickinson," she said. "Wives and children will follow me." As she escorted the group she waved at her husband who stood atop the Alamo church's walls. Almeron Dickinson served as a captain of artillery at the Alamo. He and his wife moved from Tennessee to Texas in 1831. Their daughter, Angelina, was born three years later.

Ana and her children followed Dickinson to the old sacristy room where sacred items of the church were kept and where other Tejano woman and children had sought refuge. Ana recognized Gertrudis Navarro and her sister, Juana Navarro Alsbury, among the group. Ana placed both of her hands on one of the thick stone walls. Then she bowed her head and prayed.

The interior of the roofless Alamo church was filled with a long dirt and rubble-filled ramp. At the top of the ramp were two cannons. Gregorio knew that he would probably be assigned to one of those guns.

Toribio Losoya entered the church and welcomed Gregorio.

"You made it here safely," said Toribio. "It is good to see another neighbor here at the Alamo."

"Is Abamillo here, too?" said Gregorio.

"Yes. And Seguin. And Juan Badillo and Carlos Espalier. Others, too."

"Make way!" shouted a sergeant leading a cannon crew. The group dragged the cannon slowly through the entrance to the Alamo church. The sergeant looked at the top of the gun ramp from where he stood. "All right, boys. Let's give it a try."

An artillery officer entered the church. He looked at Gregorio and Toribio. "We could use an extra set of hands."

Gregorio quickly stepped to a position on one of the gun's drag ropes. Toribio and a few other men also joined in.

"Pull!" said the officer.

The men started to pull the cannon up the ramp. It was very difficult.

"Don't stop! Keep going!" encouraged Gregorio.

The men finally pulled the cannon to the level gun platform where the two other guns had already been positioned.

Gregorio looked out at the Mexican army's camp.

"In December we tried to keep General Cós in here, and now we are in here," said Gregorio shaking his head. "We must hold out until reinforcements arrive."

"From where?" asked Juan.

"There is a sizeable force at Goliad," said Gregorio. "Colonel Fannin has several hundred volunteers at Goliad. And there are volunteers at Gonzalez and San Felipe."

"Well, they had better come quick," said Toribio. "Santa Anna has raised the flag of no quarter at the San Fernando church."

"No quarter?" questioned Gregorio.

"No prisoners. Either we defeat Santa Anna or he defeats us."

Colonel Travis called everyone into the main courtyard. Several members of the New Orleans Greys, a military unit from Louisiana, stood guard on the walls while the garrison assembled.

"All men report to your officers for your assigned positions," said Travis. "Men with families may stay with them inside the church at night. Good luck."

The 150 Alamo defenders scurried across the courtyard and regrouped near their officers. Gregorio and the other Tejanos formed next to Juan Seguin who was standing at the entrance to the corral behind the Long Barrack building.

"We all have important jobs to do," said Seguin. "You will join me as couriers for Colonel Travis. But at this time we do not have enough horses for everyone. Be ready, though, at all times. Gregorio, you will report to the artillery officer, in the church."

Travis stood at the Alamo's northwest gun platform and looked in the distance at the Mexican infantry and cavalry. Travis estimated that there were at least 1,000 of them. The Mexican soldiers started to build campfires and erect canvas tents. Dozens and dozens of tents were soon aligned in neat rows.

Travis saw the first Mexican artillery piece wheeled into position. Minutes later, it fired the first shot at the Alamo's walls. The Battle of the Alamo had begun.

CHAPTER 9

The Siege of the Alamo
February 1836

On February 24, Travis wrote a letter appealing for help.

To the people of Texas and all Americans in the world. Fellow citizens and compatriots. I am besieged by a thousand or more of the Mexicans under Santa Anna. I have sustained a continual bombardment and cannonade for 24 hours and have not lost a man. The enemy has directed a surrender at discretion, otherwise, the garrison are to be put to the sword, if the fort is taken. I have answered the demand with a cannon shot, and our flag still waves proudly from our walls. I shall never surrender or retreat. Then, I call on you in the name of Liberty, of patriotism and everything dear to the American character, to come to our aid, with all dispatch. The enemy is receiving reinforcements daily and will no doubt increase to three or four thousand in four or five days. If this call is neglected, I am determined to sustain myself as long as possible and die like a soldier who never forgets what is due to his own honor and that of his country. Victory or Death.

On the next day, the Mexicans attacked the Alamo. Several companies of soldados advanced towards the Alamo's southern defenses. Gregorio served on one of the Alamo church's cannons during the battle. The artillery fire prevented the Mexicans from reaching the Main Gate. The fighting raged for nearly two hours before Santa Anna's troops retreated.

After the fighting was over, Gregorio walked down the Alamo church's gun ramp and entered the sacristy. When he entered the room he heard his family cheer: "Happy Birthday!" He was surprised and quite pleased.

"Happy Birthday, Father," wished Enrique as he hugged Gregorio. "Happy Birthday" said his other children.

Ana kissed Gregorio. "A most Happy Birthday, my dear," said "Ana. "But I am sorry that we have nothing to give you."

Gregorio smiled as he held his wife and children. "You have given me your love," said Gregorio. "What better gift can a man receive on his birthday?"

In the days that followed, Santa Anna's army grew in size. Despite being surrounded, Travis was able to dispatch Juan Seguin and other couriers through Santa Anna's lines.

The weather was bitterly cold, especially at night. The winds whipped across the battered walls. The Alamo defenders who stood watch during the night suffered the most. On Sunday morning, February 28, the temperature was only 40 degrees. Gregorio stood by his cannon position and waited for the next command.

The sound of a horse at full gallop alerted the gun crews.

"Look," said Gregorio. "Another messenger is leaving from the corral."

The rider bolted for the alameda. At first, the Mexican sentries did not see him but soon a few musket shots rang out from their camp.

"If we fired our gun, it might divert attention away from

him," said Gregorio.

"Load!" came the command. The gun crew immediately reacted to the command.

"Prime!"

Seconds later, the gun boomed. Mexican artillery promptly returned fire.

Gregorio looked beyond the glowing Mexican campfires and saw the rider heading northeast.

"He made it!" said Gregorio. "He made it through their lines!"

Suddenly, two explosive flashes were seen at the edge of the Mexican camp opposite the east end of the Alamo. Seconds later two Mexican cannon balls smashed into the rear of the Alamo church. The powerful impact knocked Gregorio and the rest of the gun crew off their feet but they were unhurt.

Travis walked up the gun ramp and looked towards the Mexican camp. "Two new Mexican guns," said Dickinson. "If they bring in the heavy artillery they can batter this poor excuse of a fort into a pile of rubble."

"We will have to hold out until then, sir," said Gregorio.

As the day continued, the Mexican artillery kept firing. But late in the afternoon, the guns went silent. The pause in the fighting gave the defenders time to rest. Crockett took the opportunity to cheer everyone up. The famous frontiersman strutted to the center of the main courtyard and began playing his fiddle. He was quickly surrounded with cheering men, women and children who clapped and danced to his tunes. Gregorio escorted his family into the courtyard.

John McGregor, an immigrant from Scotland, soon appeared with his bagpipes. He joined Crockett in a memorable musical duet. Hardly anyone in the Alamo had ever heard bagpipes before. When McGregor first filled the bag up with his breath, the pipes made such a low squeal that some of the children placed their hands over their ears.

For a few minutes, it seemed that everyone in the Alamo had forgotten the threat that existed outside the walls. The woman and children left the confines of the Alamo church and watched Crockett and McGregor entertain the garrison. Maria took Gregorio by the hand and danced with him. Other children joined hands with them. They formed a large circle and danced to the lively music. Gregorio and Ana shared a smile for the first time in nearly a week.

Crockett and McGregor played until dark when a Mexican cannon shot put an end to the peace. All the men hurried back to their positions. The women and children sought protection in the sacristy.

A cannon duel erupted. The guns filled the night with thunderous explosions but fortunately no one was injured. After an hour, the Mexican guns stopped firing.

Gregorio ran down the gun ramp and entered the sacristy where his family was staying. The room was crowded with women and children.

"How are you doing?" asked Gregorio.

"We are safe," said Ana.

"Are you getting enough food?"

"Yes, my husband. We are all well. And you?"

"I am well," said Enrique.

Gregorio's serious look quickly dissolved into a proud smile. Enrique held up his wooden toy pistol.

"If you need me up there, I am ready," said Enrique.

"I will tell Colonel Travis of your readiness," said Gregorio.

A cannon ball smashed into the side of the church but the thick walls withstood the impact. Another shot hit moments later but only a few flakes of stone fell from the ceiling.

"You are all safe in here," said "Gregorio." "Stay here."

Gregorio ate supper with his family and then returned to his artillery position. The Mexican guns fell silent during the night. Gregorio returned to his family and was able to get several hours of sleep in the sacristy.

Just before dawn, Toribio shook Gregorio awake.

"Gregorio, Santa Anna has made an offer to Travis to surrender," whispered Toribio so he would not wake the children.

Gregorio rubbed his eyes and sat up on his elbows. Ana woke up, too.

"Surrender?" questioned Gregorio with a yawn.

"Juan said that he heard the news from someone who served as an interpreter in Santa Anna's headquarters," said Toribio. "He told me that Santa Anna may allow the Anglos to surrender but if they did we Tejanos would still be treated as rebels."

"What does that mean," asked Ana softly.

"Rebels," said Toribio. "The Tejanos would be treated as pirates."

Ana realized what Toribio meant.

"Is this true?" asked Gregorio. "Or is this another rumor?"

"It must be true," said Toribio.

"And what of the women and children?" asked Gregorio.

"Santa Anna said that they may leave."

Gregorio grabbed his wife by her shoulders and looked directly at her. "If what Toribio says is true, you must go, Ana. Take the children."

"No," said Ana. "If you are going to stay, so am I."

Gregorio held his wife in his arms. He looked down at his children.

"May God protect us all."

The story of a possible surrender agreement proved to be false. Santa Anna remained firm in his position that all of the Alamo defenders would be punished for opposing his rule. The punishment would be death.

CHAPTER 10

The Gonzales 32

March 1836

Help finally arrived at the Alamo.

Early on the morning of March 1, reinforcements approached the Alamo. Thirty-two men from Gonzales entered the main gate of the mission-fortress. The group was led by two Alamo couriers, including Gregorio's friend, John Smith. Everyone was excited that the entire group made it in safely through the Mexican lines.

Gregorio ran to his friend.

"Any casualties?' asked Gregorio.

"None," said Smith as he got off his horse.

"Excellent," said Gregorio as he looked around in the darkness. "How many in your group?"

"Thirty-two, counting myself,"

"Thirty-two? We could use ten times that number," said Gregorio. "But it is good to see you again and your fellow volunteers."

"Have you heard from your family?" asked Smith.

"They are here with me."

"Not exactly the safest place to be, do you think?"

"Ana and the children are inside the church," said Gregorio. "They are safe as long as they remain there."

Gregorio walked with Smith to the corral.

"Things are changing, Gregorio."

"What do you mean?"

"Some folks are pushing for more than rights now that Santa Anna is here."

"I fight to restore the Constitution of 1824," said Gregorio. "And so do you."

"Not any more, my friend. I fight for independence from Mexico," said Smith. "And so do many others."

"I have heard of such talk."

"It could happen," said Smith. "At least that's what some of the men from Gonzales were saying."

On the next day at Washington-on-the Brazos, an important event changed the Texas Revolution forever. No longer was it a fight to restore the rights citizens enjoyed under the Mexican Constitution of 1824. Instead, delegates from various Texas communities declared independence from Mexico.

The Texas Declaration of Independence authorized the creation of a new government. The free citizens of Texas would have the right to elect their leaders, establish public schools and provide religious freedom. The document rejected Santa Anna's dictatorship.

But news of the declaration never reached the Alamo.

On March 3, a messenger arrived at the Alamo with a letter that pledged 300 volunteers from Colonel James Fannin's command at Goliad and more men from other settlements. Travis thought that a force of over 800 Texans could effectively challenge Santa Anna's army. But they had to arrive as soon as possible.

While Travis eagerly awaited reinforcements, Santa Anna

greeted an additional 800 soldiers to his growing ranks of thousands. The Mexican Army's musicians celebrated the arrival of the soldiers by playing songs into the night.

Inside the Alamo, conditions worsened. Supplies were running low and several men were sick, including Jim Bowie.

"Colonel Bowie is very sick with the fever," said Toribio. "I heard that he may not last another day."

"Bowie is a strong man, a fighter," said Gregorio. "Do not count him out yet."

"I wonder when Fannin will get here?" asked Toribio.

"Seguin should have brought him here by now," said Juan. "Goliad is just about as far away from the Alamo as Gonzales."

"Until Fannin gets here, be prepared and stay alert," said Gregorio.

On the next day, Santa Anna called his officers to his headquarters tent for a very important meeting. He ordered an attack on the Alamo the following morning. Some of his officers asked him to wait a few more days for his largest cannons to arrive. They suggested that the Alamo could not withstand the firepower of the big artillery pieces. But Santa Anna did not want to wait any longer. He ordered his men to rest and then prepare for the attack.

Santa Anna wanted his troops to storm the Alamo in the dark of the morning just before sunrise. Santa Anna believed that most of the Alamo's defenders would be asleep. Some of the soldiers were ordered to carry ladders in order to climb the walls of the Alamo.

From Travis' view on the Alamo's north wall, all seemed particularly quiet in the Mexican camp. He ordered his sentries to keep a lookout for Fannin and his reinforcements from Goliad. But Travis realized that help probably would not reach him in time. He sent out another messenger.

The siege of the Alamo had lasted twelve days. Travis told his officers that he expected Santa Anna's heavy artillery would arrive soon. The big guns would eventually crumble the thick walls of the Alamo, even the church. Without the protection of the walls, the Alamo defenders would be doomed.

Travis asked the Alamo defenders to assemble in the main courtyard. He wanted to tell them something. His officers went to all corners of the Alamo and told the men of Travis' request.

Gregorio stood next to John Smith and Toribio. Juan stood near Davy Crockett and some of the other Tennesseans. A group of Tejanos were joined by some of the New Orleans Greys.

After the men of the Alamo lined up, Colonel Travis walked out from his headquarters room. He stood in front of the Alamo defenders.

"Fannin must be on the road from Goliad by now," said Travis. "But I fear that he may not arrive in time. The defense of the Alamo rests with us. You have held the enemy for twelve days. You have all done your duty. But it would be wrong of me to ask you to stay against such overwhelming odds. As such, any man wishing to leave may do so. But as for me, I will remain."

Travis gripped his sword and drew a line into the dirt with the weapon.

"To all those who will stand with me, cross this line."

Davy Crockett and several Tennesseans stepped forward. Gregorio crossed the line. Toribio, Juan and other Tejanos followed. Captain William Carey, who was born in Virginia, walked towards the Alamo commander. New Jersey's Richard Stockton and England's Richard Starr crossed the line, too. Soon, everyone stood next to Travis.

"Thank you, men," said Travis. The men drifted back to where they were stationed.

Gregorio walked back to the sacristy to see his family.

"I have never heard it so quiet," said Ana.

"Indeed," said Gregorio as he looked at his sleeping children. "So very quiet. Ana, I want to tell you something."

"What?" she said.

"Something very important," he said.

"What is it?" said Ana.

"Remember what you see here," said Gregorio.

"Why do you say such things, Gregorio?" she said.

"Just remember," said Gregorio.

Ana nodded as tears filled her eyes.

Gregorio walked out of the sacristy towards the gun ramp.

"Mother?" said Enrique

"I thought you were asleep," Ana said.

"Do not worry," said Enrique. "I will remember, too."

CHAPTER 11

....

The Battle of the Alamo
March 6, 1836

The predawn darkness was usually the quietest time of day. Nearly everyone was asleep. But not on the morning of March 6.

The Mexican camp was a beehive of activity. Soldiers filled their cartridge boxes and cleaned their weapons. The cavalry horses were fed. Officers organized their companies.

In town, members of Santa Anna's reserves awaited their orders. Gregorio's brother, Francisco, stood at attention in the ranks. He wondered when he would be called to join in the attack on the Alamo. Would he confront his own brother on the battlefield?

Inside the Alamo, a few men patrolled the walls. One volunteer walked along the gun platform at the north wall. A guard at the main gate struggled to stay awake.

The morning was cold and clear. In the eastern sky the first hint of light could be seen. The thirteenth day of the siege had begun.

Santa Anna placed over 1,500 soldiers in position to attack the Alamo. Some of the soldiers carried ladders so that they could climb the Alamo's walls. He wanted to make sure that the attack would be a success.

Santa Anna held a force of nearly 400 men in reserve

near his headquarters in the field. And the local reserves, including Francisco Esparza, stood by in the town. The Mexican soldiers eagerly awaited Santa Anna's signal for the attack to begin in the pre-dawn darkness.

But some of the soldiers did not wait for the bugle call. They had waited thirteen days for this moment and could not contain themselves any longer. Shouts of "Viva Santa Anna!" filled the air. The bugles sounded and the Mexican columns rushed forward.

Inside the Alamo, the defenders sprang from where they slept and ran to their assigned positions. Gregorio kissed his wife and children. Ana was too frightened to speak. Gregorio quickly followed Captain Dickinson out of the sacristy. They climbed the gun ramp and joined the other artillerists at the cannons.

"Load!" ordered Dickinson.

Gregorio and the other gunners loaded their cannons as rapidly as they could.

"Prime!"

Moments later, the first Alamo cannon shots of the battle filled the air.

At the north wall, Travis carried a shotgun and stood next to one of the other cannons. The cannon shot felled nearly an entire company of Mexican soldiers. A volley of gunfire from the darkness filled the air with smoke. Then more weapons fired. The Alamo defenders fired back. Another volley blasted away and Travis fell. The Alamo commander was one of the first defenders to die.

The Alamo's cannons continued to roar. But Mexican muskets started to take their toll on the gun crews, especially those at the north wall. The dim light of dawn allowed Gregorio to see the infantry advancing on the corral area.

Turn the gun," said Gregorio as he pointed east. Captain Dickinson and the gunners turned the cannon and fired it. Dozens of Mexican soldiers fell with the single blast. But more followed.

The firepower from the Alamo cannons and rifles was so effective that the three Mexican columns altered their attack and regrouped. Santa Anna wanted a complete victory so he sent in all his reserves, but he did not order the local reserve force in town to participate.

The Mexican officers reformed their ranks and led the charge against the north wall. Over 1,000 Mexican soldiers massed together for the assault.

Inside the sacristy, the women and children huddled together. One small candle lantern provided just enough light for Ana to see the frightened faces of her children.

Repeated Mexican musket volleys started to take their toll. Alamo defenders started to fall. One by one, the cannons on the north wall were silenced.

Finally, the Mexican soldiers reached the walls. Ladders were put in place and the soldiers began their climbs. At the top of the ladders, Alamo defenders met them with flintlock pistols, knives and tomahawks. Some defenders pushed the ladders over but the Mexican soldiers quickly repositioned them. There were too many soldiers for the Texans to contend with.

Mexican soldiers managed to climb the walls at the southwest gun platform and gain control of the Alamo's biggest cannon. Several soldiers ran down the gun ramp and opened the main gate. Mexican soldiers poured into the Alamo.

Captain Dickinson ran into the sacristy. "The Mexicans are inside our walls!" he told his wife. "If they spare you, save my child." He ran back to his position.

As the battle waged on, most of the remaining defenders sought protection in the rooms of the Long Barrack building, the west wall rooms and the church. One of the Alamo cannons was turned by the Mexican soldiers who fired it into one of the rooms. Once the door was blasted open, Mexican soldiers entered the smoke-filled room and fought the few defenders who were still alive.

Francisco Esparza heard the battle continue from his post in town. He could see clouds of gunpowder fill the sky. He wondered if Gregorio was still alive. He thought about his sister-in-law and her children.

Within an hour, Santa Anna's soldiers controlled every area of the Alamo compound except for the church. Texan and Mexican bodies filled the courtyard. A group of Mexican soldiers charged through the church's blockaded front doorway and were greeted with a blast from one of the cannons. For a moment the gunfire stopped. It was a strange silence.

Gregorio heard shouts outside the Alamo. It sounded like Texans. Had Fannin arrived? He looked over the low rear wall of the church and saw two groups of Texans running for the trees and bushes nearby. The Mexican cavalry quickly closed in on them. A few managed to fight but the long cavalry lances soon put an end to their resistance.

Gregorio, Captain Dickinson and a few defenders stood at the top of the gun platform and waited for the next charge. They were out of artillery ammunition. "Viva Santa Anna!" shouted dozens of soldiers as they rushed up the gun ramp. Gregorio fired his rifle and a soldier fell. Shots rang out and Captain Dickinson fell. A Mexican corporal lunged at Gregorio with his bayonet. Gregorio grabbed the weapon and struggled with the soldier. But other Mexican soldiers with bayonets joined in. Gregorio was struck and fell lifeless next to the cannon.

When the gunfire stopped, Santa Anna rode into the fort. Several Alamo defenders were captured and were brought before Santa Anna. The general questioned why these men were still alive. He ordered their immediate execution.

Mexican officers entered the sacristy and escorted the women and children outside. As Ana left the room she glanced at the top of the gun ramp and saw Gregorio's body. She collapsed and one of the officers helped her to her feet.

"Mother, what is wrong?" asked Enrique from the courtyard, where he stood with his sister and brothers next to Mrs. Dickinson.

"Father?" asked Enrique quietly.

"They are all gone," said Susanna Dickinson.

CHAPTER 12

....

After the Battle

March 6, 1836

Francisco Esparza walked towards the Alamo.

The local reserves were never used in the battle but Francisco wanted to see his brother.

"Where are you going?" said one of the reserves to Francisco. "The battle is over."

"I search for my brother," said Francisco.

"Why? He is dead like all the other pirates."

Francisco turned to the soldier. He was very angry.

"Don't you ever talk about my brother that way. Do you understand?"

"Yes, yes, of course," nodded the soldier.

The main road to the old mission was flanked by dozens of wounded Mexican soldiers. By the time Francisco reached the Alamo's main gate, he saw the bodies of the Alamo defenders being carted to piles of wood. One of the dead was Juan Abamillo.

"What are they doing?" asked Francisco to a soldier wearing a bloodied sling on his right arm.

"They are burning the bodies of the rebels."

Francisco ran to one of the carts which carried the bodies of eight Alamo defenders. Toribio Losoya was on the first cart. He ran to the other carts looked but could not find Gregorio's body. Then he rushed inside the compound and searched every room. He climbed the gun platforms at the southwest corner and the north wall.

He finally made his way across the courtyard where he saw Ana and the children.

"I am sorry, Ana," said Francisco. "Where is…?"

Ana pointed to the church but said nothing. Francisco walked inside the battered church's entrance and spotted his brother's body. He saw a group of soldiers lift Gregorio's body from the platform.

"Stop!" shouted Francisco as he ran up the gun ramp. "You will not burn his body."

The soldiers looked surprised.

"Since when does a reservist counter the orders of Santa Anna," laughed one of the soldiers.

"Do not touch him!" demanded Francisco.

Suddenly, Santa Anna and some officers entered the church.

"*Atención!*" shouted one of the men. Everyone snapped to attention.

"What goes on here?" said Santa Anna.

Francisco lifted Gregorio in his arms and carried him to the bottom of the gun ramp.

"He is my brother, Excellency," said Francisco. "I wish to bury him."

Santa Anna looked around at the damage and the bodies of the dead Texians.

"It was but a small affair," said Santa Anna. "Take him and go."

Later that day, Francisco buried his brother at Campo Santo, a cemetery located on the western edge of town. Ana and the children attended the simple ceremony. Maria and Enrique held their mother's hands as a priest conducted the rituals at the gravesite. "May his soul and the souls of all the faithful departed through the mercy of God rest in peace," said the priest.

"I am sorry, my brother," said Francisco as he stood by the grave. "Rest in peace."

CHAPTER 13

San Antonio 1907

Six weeks after the fall of the Alamo, General Sam Houston defeated Santa Anna at the Battle of San Jacinto on April 21, 1836. During the battle, Houston's soldiers shouted "Remember the Alamo!" As a result of the victory, Texas won its independence. From 1836 to 1845, the Republic of Texas was an independent nation. But in 1845, the citizens of Texas decided to be a part of the United States. Texas became the nation's 28th state.

The Esparza children grew up as citizens of the United States. The boys matured into young men. Each married and raised a family. Maria, though, died in 1849.

Manuel died in 1886, fifty years after the Battle of the Alamo. Francisco died the next year. But Enrique lived into the 20th century. He and his wife, Gertrudis, had five children. Enrique became the last person still living who had survived and remembered the Battle of the Alamo.

In 1907, Charles Merritt Barnes a reporter for the *San Antonio Express* interviewed Enrique at his home.

"The first thing I'd like to do is thank you for granting me this interview," said Barnes. "I'm very interested in your story. Your father fought at the Alamo. And you are the last one: the last survivor of the siege and battle of the Alamo. That was seventy-one years ago."

Enrique looked away for a moment. He looked into the sunlight shining through his only window and took a deep breath.

"Yes," said Enrique. "All the others are dead. I alone live of they who were within the Alamo when it fell. There is none other left now to tell its story."

"But do you remember the story of the Alamo?" asked Barnes.

"You ask me do I remember it," said Enrique as he sat forward in his chair. "I tell you, yes. Neither age nor infirmity could make me forget, for the scene was one of such horror that it could never be forgotten."

"Did you see your father's body after the battle?" asked Barnes.

"I did not get a chance to see it before it was buried," said Enrique.

"Did you see Santa Anna," asked Barnes.

"Yes I did," said Enrique. "Santa Anna gave my mother a blanket and two silver dollars. He gave that sum to the other women who were inside the Alamo."

Barnes continued to interview Enrique for the rest of the afternoon. He finally put down his pencil.

"You know, folks can hardly recognize the Alamo these days," said Barnes. "That big store covers up everything but the church. And the rest of Alamo Plaza is built up with all kinds of businesses and shops. If they keep building no one will be able to see the Alamo."

Enrique folded his arms and sat back in his chair.

"But we will always remember the Alamo defenders," said Barnes. "Gregorio Esparza was one of them. He was a Texas hero. You should be very proud of your father."

"Indeed," said Enrique.

"Well, it's time for me to get back to the office," said Barnes as he shook Enrique's hand. "I've got a story to write."

Barnes walked to the door. He stopped and turned.

"Oh, just one more thing, Mr. Esparza: did your father leave you anything from the battle? Anything at all?"

"No, nothing remains," said Enrique.

"I thought there might have been something."

"Only the memories, Mr. Barnes," said Enrique. "And when I go to sleep my last slumber in the Campo Santo, there will be no one left to tell the story."

"I am sure that your children and grandchildren will tell the story."

"I am sure they will."

"Again, I thank you," said Barnes.

As Barnes stood in the doorway, he looked around the room and noticed a small wooden object resting on a table. It looked like a toy pistol.

GLOSSARY

Alameda   A tree lined area.

Amigo   Spanish for friend.

Artillery   Weapons, like cannons, which fire projectiles.

Cavalry   Mounted soldiers who fight on horseback.

Constitution   A system of principles upon which a nation is governed.

Couriers   Messengers.

Fandango   A dance or festival.

Flintlock pistol   A hand gun that used flint to ignite its gunpowder charge.

Garrison   A group of soldiers stationed at a particular place like a fort.

Gunner   An artillerist. One who helps load and fire a cannon.

Infantry   Soldiers who fight on foot.

Linstock   An artillery tool which held the ignited match that fired the cannon.

Musket   A muzzle-loaded, smooth-bore (not rifled) shoulder weapon.

Sacristy   A room inside a church where scared items are kept.

Sponge-ram staff	A two-ended artillery tool used to swab out the cannon barrel and ram down the gunpowder and projectile charge.
Tejano	An Hispanic/Latino resident of early Texas.
Texian	An Anglo-American resident of early Texas.
Thumbstall	A thumbcover used by artillerists to close the touchhole on a cannon.
Touch hole	A tiny opening near the top of a cannon barrel where the gunpowder was ignited.
Treason	A crime of disloyalty against one's country.
Volley	Simultaneous firing of weapons.

INDEX